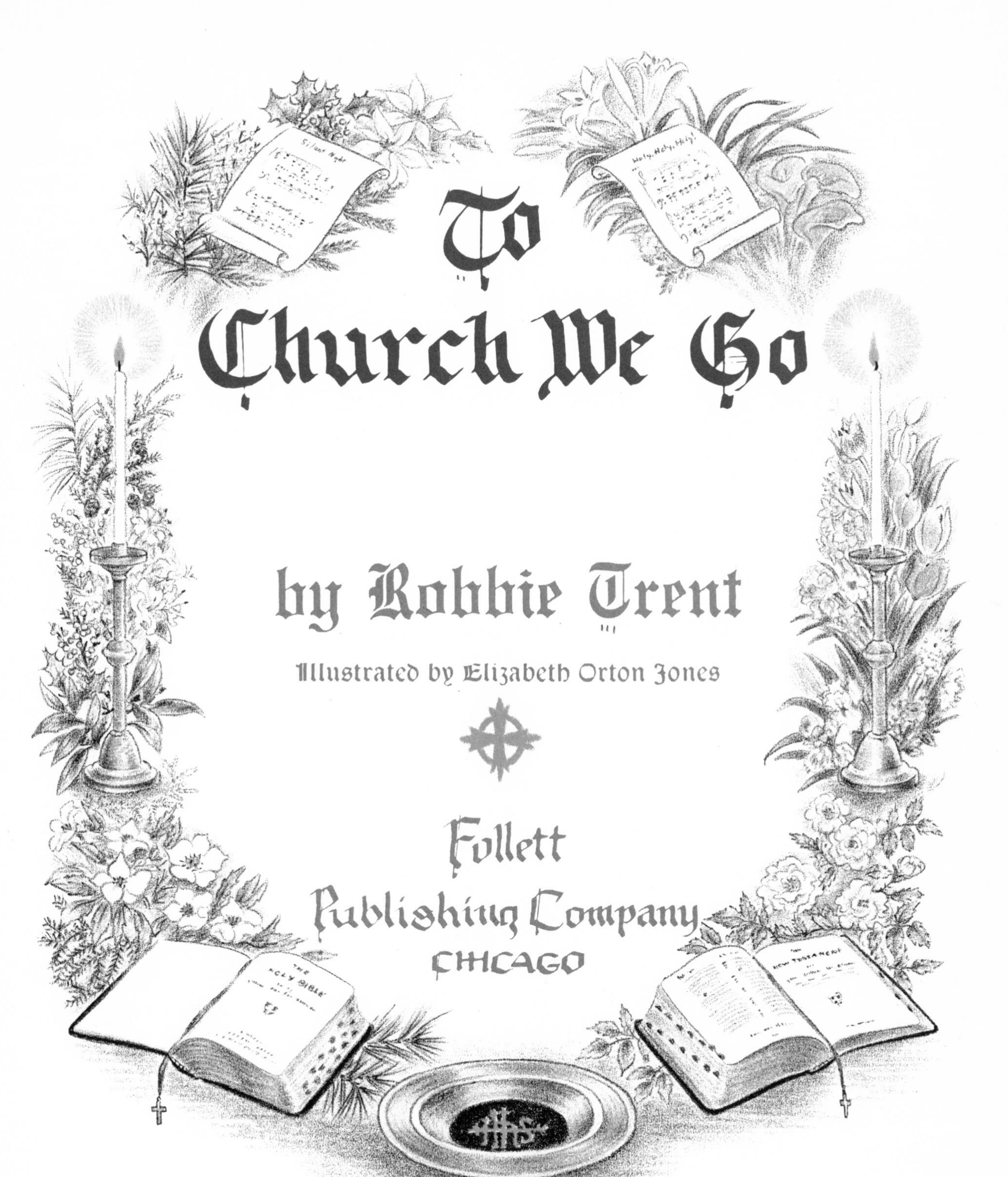

To Church We Go

by Robbie Trent

Illustrated by Elizabeth Orton Jones

Follett
Publishing Company
CHICAGO

TO CHURCH WE GO, by Robbie Trent

MANUFACTURED IN THE UNITED STATES OF AMERICA
Published simultaneously in Canada
by Ambassador Books, Limited

Library of Congress Catalog Card Number: 56-11219

TO CHURCH WE GO
BY ROBBIE TRENT
·WELCOME·

All over our land there are churches. There are churches in big cities and in quiet country places. There are churches in little towns and far out on the plains. In our world there are more than a million churches.

Some churches are built of red brick or gray stone. Others are made of wood and painted white. Some churches are made of yellow mud or dried grasses. Others are tents made of strong cloth.

All of these churches are alike in one way. Each church has been built as a special place. Each church has one great purpose. Each church invites boys and girls and men and women to meet together and do one special thing.

O come, let us worship and bow down; let us kneel before the Lord our maker.

On Sunday we have a happy feeling of a day that is different. We put on fresh clothes. We go with our family and friends to church. We are going to worship God.

I was glad when they said unto me, Let us go into the house of the Lord.

At church there is friendliness. We smile and share our books. We are polite and kind. We are learning to be friendly.

Peace be to thee . . . . Greet the friends by name.
Be gentle unto all.

In church we sit quietly and think of God. Sometimes the stillness goes deep down inside us. Our minds are quiet too. We think, and we remember.

Be still and know that I am God.

At church we pray to God. We talk with the Heavenly Father. Sometimes the prayers are praises to God. We say, "Thank you, God."

Sometimes the prayers are "I'm sorry" prayers. We say, "Forgive me, please." Sometimes the prayers ask for help. We say, "*What time I am afraid, I will trust in thee.*"

We pray for ourselves. We pray for our friends. We pray for people whom we do not know. "Bless them," we pray, "and help us to love all people."

Cause me to hear thy lovingkindness in the morning;
for in thee do I trust . . . Teach me to do thy will;
for thou art my God.

In church we are glad for Jesus, our friend. We think of a day long ago. The mothers were bringing their children to Jesus. "Stop," some-one said. "Jesus is busy."

But Jesus loved the children. He took them in his arms. He gave them his blessing. We remember Jesus' words.

Suffer the little children to come unto me,
and forbid them not:
for of such is the kingdom of God.

At church we listen to words from the Bible. Sometimes there are stories of Jesus and his friends. Sometimes the story is about a grain of wheat or two sparrows. Sometimes there are stories of long-ago people who knew God.

Often there are Bible poems that sound like music. Sometimes there are verses we know. We hear, *"The Lord is good to all."* We remember, *"Be ye kind one to another."*

*Blessed are they that hear the word of God
and keep it.*

ST. MATTHEW
31 Fear ye not therefore,
ye are of more value
than many sparrows.
16
17

Sometimes music helps us to worship God at church. When the sounds are soft and quiet, they say, *"Thou art near, O Lord."* When the notes are gay and happy, they say: *"Make a joyful noise unto the Lord." "Thou hast put gladness into my heart."* When the tones are slow and deep, they say, *"Great is our Lord, and of great power."*

Praise ye the Lord . . . Praise him with stringed instruments and organs.

Sometimes there are flowers at church. There are green plants growing. Sometimes soft colors are shining in a window. There are long shadows on the floor.

We think of God who made flowers and herbs. We think of God who gives each growing thing its own kind of beauty. We think of God who planned for light and color. And we worship.

I will praise thy name;
for thou hast done wonderful things.

Thou art the God that doest wonders.

At church we sing glad songs. All the people sing. Together we make music to God. We sing unto the Lord.

Sometimes there are two songs at the same time. There is the quiet singing inside us. There are the words our lips say. We are praising God with our song.

I will praise the Lord with my whole heart.
My mouth shall praise thee with joyful lips.
I will sing unto the Lord.

We worship God in bringing gifts to church. These gifts are our offerings.

We put our money together at church. We ask God to bless our gifts. We ask him to bless all people.

We thank God that our gifts can help people who are hungry and people who are sick. We thank him that they can help to tell our neighbors and our faraway friends about Jesus.

When we bring offerings to church, we are helping in work that God wants done, and God is pleased. He is pleased with the offerings of those who are just and kind.

Bring an offering and come before him:
worship the Lord in the beauty of holiness.

At church we listen to wise people. We remember things our mothers have told us to do. We think of words our fathers have said. Sometimes we think new thoughts.

As we listen, we decide to make people happy every day. We will touch small creatures gently. We will ask lonely children to play with us. We will share our skates and our food.

Let us love one another: for love is of God.

At church we think about people of many places and many races. We remember that God's love is big enough for all of them. We think of friends with brown faces and with yellow faces, with black faces and with white faces. We remember friends in lands across the seas.

We worship God with good will to all people. We worship God in seeking good for all people. Planning and working for good for all people is a part of Christian love. And Christian love can make a good world.

Have we not all one father?
Hath not one God created us?

God that made the world and all things therein . . .
hath make of one blood all nations of men.

At church we learn to live. We learn to live more pleasantly at home. We learn to live more happily in our neighborhood. We learn to live more helpfully with people all over the world.

Be ye doers of the word, and not hearers only.

When church is over we stand together. We close our eyes, and bow our heads to receive the benediction.

The benediction is a special prayer that asks God to bless us and to take care of us through all the hours of the day, through all the days of our lives.

The Lord bless thee, and keep thee: The Lord make his face shine upon thee, and be gracious unto thee: The Lord lift up his countenance upon thee, and give thee peace.